HEIKO ANTONIEWICZ

MOLECULAR BASICS

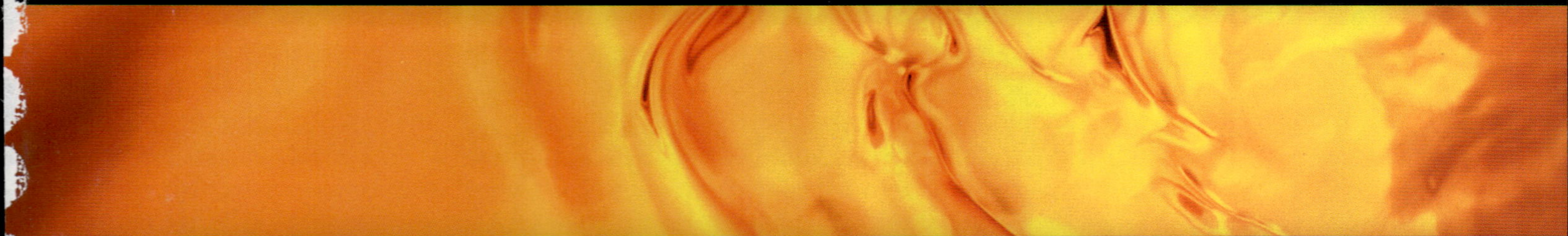

FUNDAMENTAL PRINCIPLES AND RECIPES

MATTHAES VERLAG GMBH

CONTENTS

"Taste is the sum of quality, experience and imagination"

Heiko Antoniewicz

Dear friends of innovative cuisine

This book and the texturePro® Professional Food Texturizer Kit give you the unique opportunity to try out 50 professional recipes with 10 first-class texturizers. The combination makes it easy to step into the new world of molecular cuisine, bringing entirely new facets everyday products.

Taste is the sum of quality, experience and imagination. You, too, can develop and discover an entirely new variety of tastes and amazingly pleasurable tastes.

texturePro products are of extremely high quality and are perfect for using in many different ways. My experience as a professional chef, during which I worked with molecular techniques for many years, combined with the expertise developed by Biozoon Food Innovations GmbH are the perfect basis for amazing results. The recipes are not just here to be duplicated; I see them more as a way of bring your own imagination to life. The book provides extensive basic facts and information about the products to be used as well as clear descriptions of the various techniques and the correct way to use the texturizers.

Good luck and, just as importantly, have fun on your journey through the world of molecular cuisine.

Heiko Antoniewicz

Application Table

Category	Product	Texturizer characteristic	Gelling property	Combination of more than one agent
Liquid drops, capsules	Algizoon®	Capsules with liquid core	In the presence of calcium	Calazoon for the calcium bath
Foams	Celluzoon®	Stable foam from a cold basis	Gels hot	Xanthazoon stops the precipitation of liquid
	Xanthazoon®	Large-pored foam: however, fairly unstable	By heating – in combination with Locuzoon	n/a
	Iotazoon®	Compact milk foams for desserts	In the presence of calcium (e.g. the calcium in milk)	Xanthazoon increases the stability and denseness of the foam
	Emulzoon®	Airy foam	Does not gel	n/a
Firm jellies	Agazoon®	Firmness of jellies according to dosage	By heating (<100 °C)	n/a
	Gellazoon low®	Firmness of jellies according to dosage	By heating (<100 °C)	Elasticity can be optimised via the dosage and/or in combination with Agazoon or Locuzoon
Thickeners	Guarzoon®	Holds particles in suspension	Does not gel	n/a
	Locuzoon®	Creamy structure, improves spreadability (milk products and fruit preparations)	By heating – with Xanthazoon	Flexible jellies are created in combination with Xanthazoon when heated for a short period
	Xanthazoon®	Gives a creamy mouth feel: for transparent liquids with particles in suspension	By heating – in combination with Locuzoon	See Locuzoon, Celluzoon, and Iotazoon

Stability with heat	Stability with acid	Stability with alcohol	Equipment and utensils required	Further instructions
++	–	+	Deep spoons, syringe or dropper, sieve (www.biozoon.de/shop)	Mineral water with a low calcium content (<60 mg/l) is best for making a basic solution
+	++	+	Cream siphon or electric whisk	After the Celluzoon solution has been mixed in, other liquids can only be whisked in cold. The foam can then be heated
+	++	+	Cream siphon or electric whisk	n/a
–	–	+	Cream siphon	The higher the fat content of the milk, the denser the foam
–	+	+	Milk frother or electric whisk	Emulzoon can also be used as a classic thickener to bind oily and aqueous phases. Example: stir 2 spoons Emulzoon into 4ml water, then stir in approx. 60ml olive oil
++	++	+	n/a	Stir into a cold medium, then heat
+	–	+	n/a	Stir into a cold medium, then heat
–	+	+	n/a	Delays formation of ice particles during the freezing process
+	+	+	n/a	Stops the precipitation of water after heating
++	+	+	n/a	n/a

n/a not applicable – not good, only a little + good ++ very good

AGAZOON
ALGIZOON
CALAZOON
CELLUZOON
EMULZOON
GELLAZOON LOW
GUAR ZOON
IOTAZOON
LOCUZOON
XANTHAZOON

SPHERIFICATION

Pearls, spheres, liquid drops, caviar...

Spheres go by many names indeed! The variety of applications is as myriad as the words themselves: balsamic vinegar drops, Greek yoghurt spheres, Aperol caviar to name but a few. What was once liquid is now firm, but only as firm as the creator chooses.

Algizoon

Recipe for a basic Algizoon solution

200ml still water | 6 flattened spoons Algizoon

Whisk the powder into the water and allow to stand until the whipped-in air has escaped. N.B.: The calcium concentration in the water needs to be below 60 mg/l.

The gelling agent Algizoon is an alginate found in the cell walls of brown algae. It is an acknowledged safe food additive that represents no health hazard.

Heiko Antoniewicz uses Algizoon in creative cuisine for gelification, spherification and to make espumas.

When an Algizoon solution drops into a Calazoon solution, it instantly turns into a gel known as a liquid drop. The outside may be a gel but the inside is a liquid, and these spheres burst in the mouth to release the flavourful liquid inside. The taste is incredibly intensive. All kinds of aromas can be encapsulated this way, either as tiny pearls or in large balls. The longer the pearls or balls lay in the calcium solution, or the longer they are stored, the thicker the gel will become. The taste is particularly intensive when the gel is thin.

Algizoon is highly sensitive to anything acid! This means that when it comes into contact with, for instance, lemon juice, vinegar or a wine reduction, the Algizoon will immediately gel with these liquids making a further reaction with the calcium impossible. The optimal ph-value is between 4 and 7. Algizoon and Calazoon together create strong gels. These are very flexible, heat-stable and can be warmed.

Calazoon

Recipe for a basic Calazoon solution

130ml still water | 5 flattened spoons Calazoon

Whisk the powder into the water.

Calazoon is simply calcium lactate, a salt created when lactic acid reacts with calcium carbonate, and is found in milk. Algizoon and Iotazoon react with calcium lactate. The concentration of the calcium is of paramount importance for many applications, for instance in the creation of liquid drops; the calcium concentration in Calazoon lies between 4 and 5%. This high concentration of the calcium influences the reaction rate at which perfectly round drops are created.

Reverse spherification needs Calazoon. The calcium content of foodstuffs already containing calcium, such as mozzarella, is increased as their calcium content is not high enough. The mixture is gelled in an Algizoon solution. Reverse spherification can also be used for fruit juice, for instance. The advantage is that the gelling process is halted immediately when the liquid drops are washed: the gelling process does not continue.

Calazoon is neutral in taste and is an acknowledged safe food additive. In fact it provides the body with the calcium it needs for building strong bones and teeth.

Recipe for a basic Algizoon solution

This is the basic recipe for many Algizoon applications. It can be made in advance and stored in the fridge for several days.

1

Prepare 200ml still water (calcium concentration below 50mg/l) and the Algizoon.

2

Whisk 6 flattened spoons Algizoon into the water.

3

Blend the Algizoon into the water thoroughly with a hand blender.

4

Allow the solution to stand to allow the whipped-in air to escape.

5

Basic Algizoon solution is finished.

Recipe for a basic Calazoon solution

This solution is uncomplicated to make and forms the basis for many applications.

1

Prepare 130ml still water.

2

Whisk 5 flattened spoons Calazoon into the water.

3

Blend the Calazoon into the water thoroughly with a hand blender.

4

Basic Calazoon solution is finished.

Aperol caviar

Aperol caviar looks really nice and is delicious. It makes a delightful aperitif added to sparkling wine or orange juice and a fantastic dessert when served with filleted orange segments.

1

Measure off 40ml Aperol.

2

Measure out 10ml Algizoon solution and mix into the Aperol.

3

Allow the Aperol-Algizoon to stand to allow the whipped-in air to escape.

4

Draw this solution into a syringe.

5

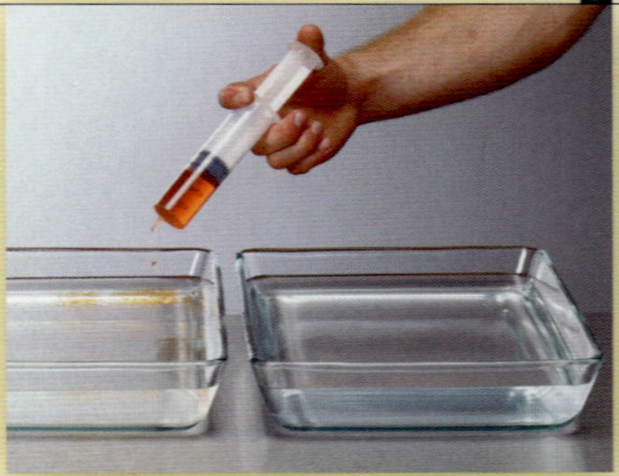

Pour some Calazoon solution (page 13) into a flat dish and dribble the Aperol solution into the Calazoon solution.

6

Allow the caviar to remain in the Calazoon solution for 30 seconds and then scoop out into plain water.

7

The Aperol caviar is complete.

Carrots spheres

1

Measure off 250ml carrot juice.

2

Measure off 35g Algizoon solution and whisk into the carrot juice.

3

Allow the mixture to stand to allow the whipped-in air to escape.

4

Whisk 5 flattened spoons Calazoon into 700ml still water. Now form spheres out of the carrot juice mass with a scoop and place in the Calazoon solution.

5

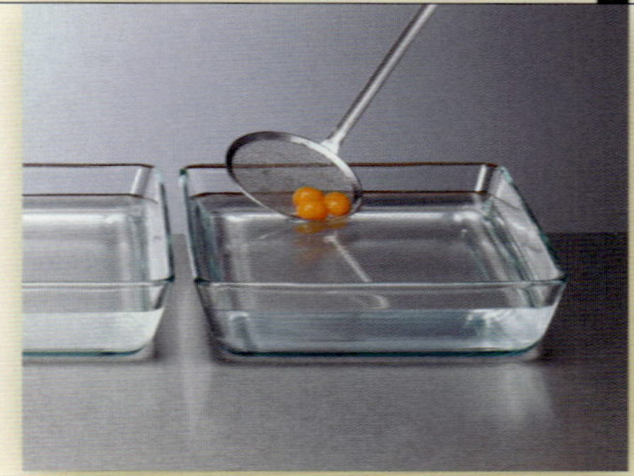

Remove the spheres after one minute and rinse in clear water.

6

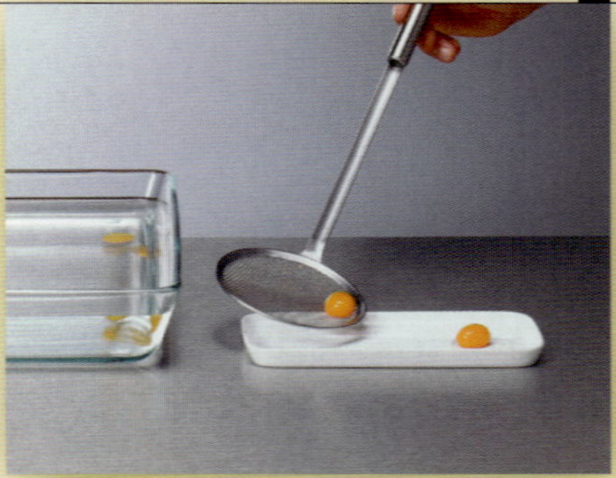

Serve the carrot spheres.

7

Firm on the outside, liquid on the inside. A perfect result!

Filled Greek yoghurt spheres

Foodstuffs already containing calcium can be made into spheres using reverse spherification by adding Calazoon. An Algizoon solution is used as a reaction bath.

1

Whisk 8 flattened spoons of Algizoon into 1 l water.

2

Mix well and allow to stand for several hours.

3

Whisk together 250g Greek yoghurt, 70g full-fat milk and 35g honey.

4

Add 4 flattened spoons of Calazoon.

5

Mix well and allow to stand to allow the whipped-in air to escape.

6

Place flat spoonfuls of yoghurt in the Algizoon solution.

7

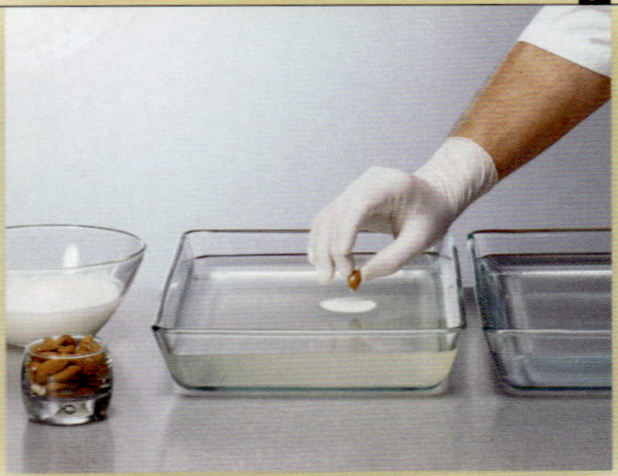

Press an almond into the yoghurt.

8

Close the sphere carefully and allow to rest for 5 to 8 minutes.

9

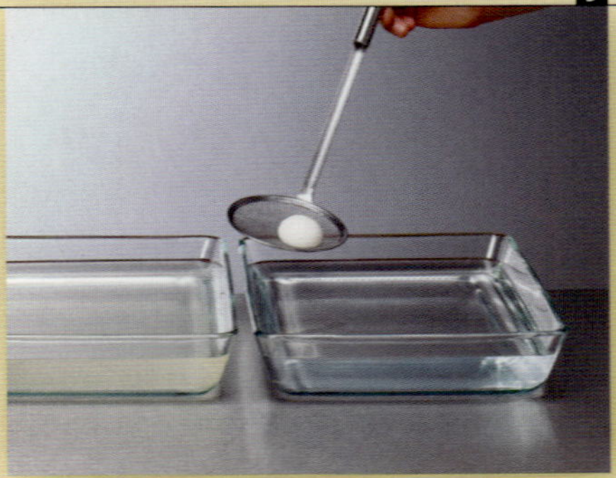

Rinse the yoghurt spheres in clear water.

10

The filled yoghurt spheres are ready.

Tomato sheets

Uncomplicated sheets can be achieved when Algizoon and Calazoon are combined. As the gelling process has been stopped, the sheets can be easily heated without them losing their form.

1

Mix 600ml tomato juice and 20ml tomato vinegar.

2

Add 14 flattened spoons Algizoon.

3

Whisk everything together and allow to stand to allow the whipped-in air to escape.

4

Pour the tomato mixture onto a platter or a flat dish.

5

Spread evenly over the surface.

6

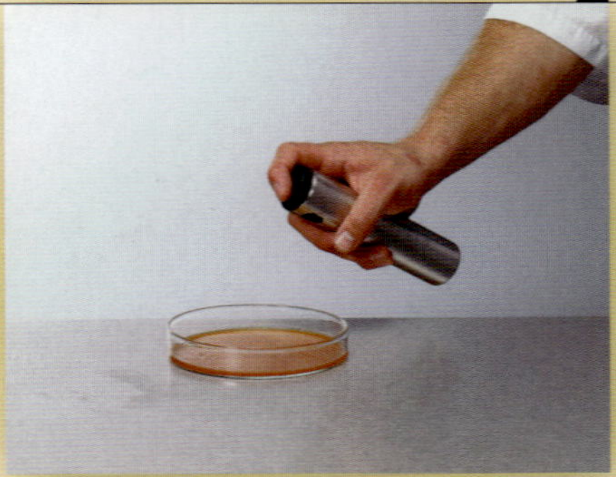

Whisk 15 flattened spoons of Calazoon into 130ml mineral water, fill into an atomizer and spray the tomato mixture well.

7

Allow the tomato sheet to stand for about 8 hours, then rinse well. There you have a tomato sheet!

Cauliflower spheres

There are several ways of creating spheres. This is how to first make a light and airy mass with an iSi Siphon and then spray the mass into a Calazoon solution.

1

Put 150g cooked cauliflower, 250ml cooking water from the cauliflower and 15ml olive oil into a Thermomix.

2

Add 5 flattened spoons Algizoon and mix until an homogenous mass has been achieved.

3

Pour into a 0.5 liter iSi siphon, screw on a charger and store in the fridge.

4

Whisk 20 flattened spoons Calazoon into 500ml water until dissolved. Create long fingers of the cauliflower masse in the Calazoon solution.

5

Cut these cauliflower fingers into pieces and allow to stand for about 5 minutes.

6

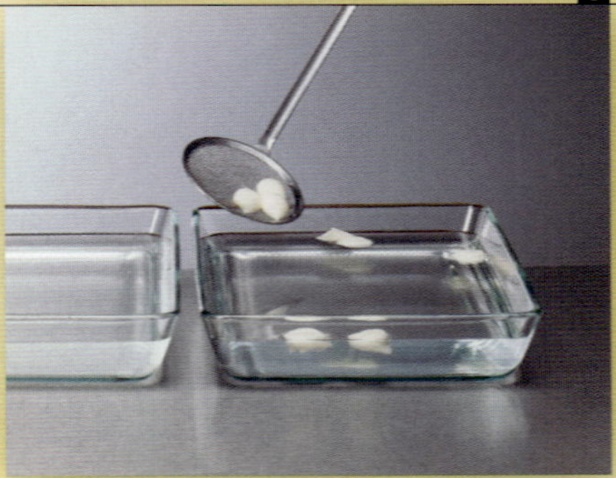

Remove the cauliflower spheres and rinse in clear water.

7

There you have cauliflower spheres.

Strawberry jam with cardamom and mint

110g strawberry juice | 40g sugar | 4 flattened spoons Algizoon | 200g strawberry dice | 1 stalk mint | 3g cardamom, ground | Brioche, fried in butter

Mix the strawberry juice, the sugar and Algizoon together, then add the diced strawberries, and bring to the boil once. Cut the mint leaves into thin juliennes and mix into the strawberry mixture with the cardamom. Pour into glass jars immediately and seal well.

Serve with brioche fried in butter.

Balsamic vinegar spheres with olive oil

Balsamic vinegar spheres

20 flattened spoons Algizoon | 1000ml still mineral water | 200ml balsamic vinegar | 3tbsp dark sugar beet syrup | 25 flattened spoons Calazoon | 50ml olive oil

Add the balsamic vinegar to 300ml still mineral water, then stir in the Algizoon. Bring to the boil, add the sugar beet syrup, bring back to the boil. Remove from the heat and allow to cool. Dissolve the Calazoon in 700ml still mineral water. Now add the balsamic vinegar mixture with a flat spoon to the Calazoon solution, allowing spheres to form. Draw the olive oil into a small syringe, add a needle and inject a little olive oil into each sphere. Turn each sphere at once so that the surface closes immediately. Let the spheres lie in the solution for 1 minute then remove and rinse in clear water. Remove from the water just before serving and pat dry.

To serve

Diced olives, marinated in olive oil | 4 anchovy fillets, cut into strips | Thyme flowers

Place the olive dice on a dish, lay the balsamic vinegar spheres on top and cover with the anchovy strips. Garnish with thyme flowers.

Carrot spheres with Ducca

Carrot spheres

500ml carrot juice | 70ml Algizoon solution | 1 drop rice vinegar | 25 flattened spoons Calazoon | 700ml still mineral water | 80g carrot julienne | 20g chervil | 15ml almond oil | 5ml rice vinegar

Whisk together 200ml carrot juice, the Algizoon solution, salt and the rice vinegar and allow to stand. In a second beaker whisk the Calazoon into the mineral water and allow to stand. Scoop small portions of the carrot juice mixture into the Calazoon solution with a flat spoon. Remove the resulting spheres and rinse these in the remaining carrot juice that has been thinned with water. Marinade the carrot julienne with chervil, almond oil, rice vinegar and salt.

To serve

Carrot purée with ginger | Almond oil | Ducca

Heat the carrot spheres in the carrot juice at 60 °C. Place the carrot purée on a plate, top with the carrot julienne and the carrot spheres. Drizzle with almond oil and a sprinkling of Ducca.

Tomato sheet with goat's milk cream cheese

Tomato sheet

600ml tomato juice | 20ml tomato vinegar | 14 flattened spoons Algizoon | 5 flattened spoons Calazoon | 100ml still mineral water

Whisk the cold tomato juice, tomato vinegar and Algizoon together and allow to stand to allow the whipped-in air to escape. Stir the Calazoon into the still mineral water, then fill this solution into an atomizer. Pour a thin film of the tomato mixture onto a sheet and spray thoroughly with the Calazoon solution. Allow to stand in the fridge for at least 8 hours until it is a firm gel, then rinse with mineral water.

Goat's milk cream cheese

200g goat's milk cream cheese | 50 crème fraîche | 1 drop vinegar | 10ml basil oil

Mix all the ingredients together, season with salt and pepper and keep in the fridge until required.

To serve

Tomato fillets confit | Pine nuts

Pipe the goat's milk cream cheese onto the tomato sheets with a piping bag, roll these up and cut into slices. Serve on a plate, alternating the tomato filets with the slices of filled tomato sheets.

Greek yoghurt with kumquats

Yoghurt

200g Greek yoghurt | 70g full-fat milk | 35g honey | 4 flattened spoons Calazoon | 8 flattened spoons Algizoon | 1l water

Whisk the yoghurt, full-fat milk, honey and Calazoon together and allow to stand to allow the whipped-in air to escape. Stir the Algizoon into the water, mix well and allow to stand for several hours.

Form yoghurt spheres from the Calazoon mixture using a flat spoon in the Algizoon solution, leaving them there for at least 5 minutes. Take care to keep the spheres separate from one another otherwise they will not form properly. Rinse the spheres in clear water.

Kumquats

100ml water | 50g sugar cane syrup | 2g Kashmir curry | Lemon zest | Saffron threads | 10 kumquats

Mix the water with the sugar cane syrup, curry, lemon zest and saffron and boil up once. Prick the kumquats all over, put into the liquid and allow to marinate for at least 12 hours. Remove when required, binding the liquid with a little Algizoon solution (page 12).

To serve

Saffron threads | Flaked almonds | Mint tips

Pat the yoghurt spheres dry and place on a plate. Garnish with the saffron threads, almonds and kumquats. Mix some smaller yoghurt spheres with the almonds, mint and saffron threads. Drizzle with a little marinade.

FOAMS

Light and airy, a mouth full of nothing but an incredible taste. Special equipment is needed to make perfect foams: a liquidizer, hand blender and a siphon. All the creator needs to make delicious, delightful pear mousseline, coffee froth, cranberry air and buttermilk lassi.

Celluzoon

Celluzoon, basically cellulose derived from plant fibers, is an indigestible dietary fiber that is completely safe to use. Liquids need only very small amounts of Celluzoon to become foams that stay stable for a long time. Large-pored, airy foams are created when the mixture is whipped up in a liquidizer: compact, creamy foams with a siphon.
Heiko Antoniewicz recommends using Celluzoon with Xanthazoon to improve water binding.
Celluzoon is easily dissolved in hot water but should always be mixed first into cold water and then brought to the boil in order to achieve the best results.
Celluzoon tolerates high salt and acid concentrations.

Emulzoon

Emulzoon is an emulsifier i.e. it allows water to be mixed with fat. Emulzoon is made from soybean oil, is registered in the EU as a food additive (also for organic foodstuffs) and is entirely safe to use. In fact, it even has anti-oxidative properties.

Heiko Antoniewicz uses Emulzoon a great deal. For instance to create ice cream, oily dressings or mayonnaise, but also for creating extremely light and fluffy foams, so-called airs. These are made by stirring Emulzoon into a liquid, either hot or cold, with a hand blender, beating the liquid until it is foamy and then spooning off the resulting froth from the surface.

This process can be continually repeated.

Iotazoon

Iotazoon is a gelling and thickening agent derived from carrageen, a polysaccharide extracted from red seaweeds. It is an acknowledged food additive with no maximum permissible quantity restrictions.

Iotazoon is used in the production of milk foams that are as smooth as cream. The higher the fat content of the milk used, the denser the milk foam. In the production of ice cream, Iotazoon makes the mass creamier and stable even it stands for quite some time – the ingredients do not separate. It would not be possible to make a warm mayonnaise without Iotazoon.

Xanthazoon

Basic recipe for a Xanthazoon solution

100ml still water | 2 flattened spoons Xanthazoon

Whisk the water and powder together.

Xanthazoon contains xanthan, a natural thickening and stabilizing agent. It is made by a fermentation process involving a special bacteria and sucrose products such as cornmeal, is entirely natural and is an acknowledged safe food additive. It is also acknowledged for use in organic food products.

Xanthazoon is an indigestible dietary fiber and can act as a laxative if consumed in large amounts. Its emulsifying properties are what make it so special for the creation of foams. The high-volume foam is very creamy and has a fantastic mouth feel. An exciting use of Xanthazoon is to bind carbon dioxide into foams and jellied liquids!

Xanthazoon is stable over a range of acidity values, dissolves easily in both hot and cold liquids and is neutral in taste.

Pear mousseline

Pear mousseline is very stable. It is best to serve it in small glass dishes. Portions are easy to create as the mixture is in an iSi siphon.

1

Mixml 350 pear juice with 20ml Williams Pear schnaps.

2

Add 2 flattened spoons Xanthazoon.

3

Whisk together with an hand blender.

4

Fill the mixture into a 0.5 litre iSi siphon, screw on a charger and store in the fridge.

5

Spray into a dish.

6

There you have your pear mousseline.

Passion fruit crème

This passion fruit crème is wonderfully thick and creamy. The Celluzoon makes the mixture very stable and it can be heated – even in the microwave.

1

Measure off 100ml.

2

Dissolve 6 flattened spoons Celluzoon in the water.

3

Mix until creamy with the hand blender.

4

Cool the Celluzoon solution down to 4 °C and allow to stand for several hours.

5

The mixture becomes clear during this period.

6

Add 35g of this Celluzoon solution to 175ml of the passion fruit mixture.

7

Beat the passion fruit mixture until creamy.

8

There you have your passion fruit foam!

Cranberry air

The cranberry air tastes sweet and tart at the same time. The fluffiness brings out the taste to an incredible degree.

1

Mix 100ml cranberry juice with 20ml cranberry syrup.

2

Add 2 flattened spoons Emulzoon.

3

Whip until light and airy with the hand blender.

4

Allow the mixture to sit for a moment or two, then scoop off the cloud and serve.

Pear mousseline with fried pear

Birnenmousseline

Pear mousseline | 350ml pear juice | 1 sprig rosemary | 2 flattened spoons Xanthazoon | 20ml Williams Pear schnaps

Heat some of the juice with the rosemary, then let it infuse for 30 minutes. Allow to cool, strain. Add the remaining juice, the Xanthazoon, the Williams Pear schnaps and pour into a 0.5 litre iSi siphon. Screw on a charger and allow to stand for 30 minutes. Spray into a dish to serve.

Fried pear

1 pear | 50ml white wine | 30g sugar | Seeds of a vanilla pod | Zest of 1/2 a lemon | 1/2 a flattened spoon Xanthazoon | 20g butter

Peel the pear and cut off four even slices. Dice the rest. Bring the white wine and sugar to the boil, add the vanilla seeds and lemon zest, and bind with the Xanthazoon. Add the diced pear and allow to poach until soft. Fry the pear slices in the butter with the vanilla seeds, maybe adding a little sugar. Glaze lightly.

To serve

Pistachio paste | Chopped pistachios | Dried cranberries, diced

Draw a decorative line on a plate with the pistachio paste. Lay the pear slices on the line. Add the diced pear, the chopped pistachios and the cranberries. Spray the mousseline into a separate glass dish and serve.

Scallops with raspberry vinaigrette

Raspberry vinaigrette

30ml raspberry vinegar | 10ml raspberry syrup | 20ml chicken stock | 20ml rape-seed oil | 10g chervil, chopped | 1 flattened spoon Emulzoon

Blend all the ingredients together and season with salt

To serve

8 scallops | Olive oil | 2 raspberries | 1 clove garlic | Zest of 1/2 a lemon

Slice 4 of the scallops, season lightly with salt and allow to marinate in the raspberry vinaigrette. Fry the remaining scallops in the olive oil for 1 minute on each side. Cut the raspberries into quarters. Slice the garlic very finely on a slicer and fry in plenty of oil. Drain well on kitchen paper and then place on the fried scallops with the raspberries. Sprinkle with lemon zest and serve.

Banana with coffee froth

Banana 4 mini bananas | Zest of 1/2 a lime | Pinch Ras al Hanout | 1tsp acacia honey | 1tsp yuzu | 10g butter

Put the peeled mini bananas, lime zest, Ras al Hanout, acia honey and yuzu in a plastic vacuum pouch, vacuum seal and poach in a water bath for 20 minutes at 62 °C. Reduce the liquor a little, bind with butter and use to glaze the bananas. Cut into evenly sized pieces. Sprinkle some of the pieces with brown sugar and caramelize.

Coffee froth 500ml cream | 300g coffee beans | 100g sugar | Pinch of anise, ground | Pinch of cardamom, ground | Seeds of a vanilla pod | 1 flattened spoon Xanthazoon

Heat the cream to 60 °C, add the coffee beans and allow them to draw for about 20 minutes. Whisk in the sugar, anise, cardamom, vanilla seeds and the Xanthazoon. Pour into an iSi siphon and keep in the fridge until required.

To serve Coffee sauce | Banana purée | 1 mini banana, sliced lengthwise | Atsina cress

Draw a line across a plate with the coffee sauce and lay the banana purée on it. Roll up the slices of mini banana, fill with coffee froth and garnish with cress. Lay a few glazed and caramelized banana pieces on the side and serve.

Curry bread with mango chutney

Curry bread

450g flour | 3tsp brown cane sugar | 18g fresh yeast | 100ml lukewarm water | 2 flattened spoons Xanthazoon | 90ml banana juice | 1tbsp olive oil | 1tsp salt | 2tsp Thai yellow curry paste | 1tsp rice vinegar

Sieve the flour into a large bowl, sprinkle with the brown cane sugar. Make a well in the center and crumble in the yeast. Stir in 7 tablespoons water. Sprinkle a little flour over the top and allow to stand in a warm place for 15 minutes. Whisk the Xanthazoon into the remaining water. Mix this solution with the banana juice, the olive oil, salt, curry paste and rice vinegar, then mix the whole lot into the yeast starter. Knead until the dough is smooth. Continue to knead well until the dough has become elastic and is no longer sticky. Cover and leave in a warm place for 20 to 30 minutes until double in size.

Roll out the dough 8 mm thick, cut into strips 25 cm long and bake for about 8 minutes at 200 °C. The bread can also be baked in any kind or shape of baking tin but the baking time must be adjusted accordingly.

Mango chutney

1/2 a mango | 2tbsp mango purée | A little mineral water | Zest of 1 lemon | 1tsp fresh coriander, chopped | 1 pinch coriander seed, finely ground

Cut the mango into small dice. Bring the mango purée to the boil with the mineral water and quickly poach the diced mango. Season with the lemon zest and coriander.

To serve A few mango slices | Shiso cress | Strips of fresh chili

Lay a few mango slices on a plate, spoon some mango chutney on top and garnish with the chili strips and shiso cress. Lay the bread sticks on the side.

Buttermilk lassi with cherries

Buttermilk lassi

200ml buttermilk | 30g sugar | Zest of 1/2 a lime | 2 flattened spoons Iotazoon

Whisk the buttermilk, sugar, lime zest and Iotazoon together. Keep in the fridge until required.

Cherries

100g sweet cherries | 20ml cane sugar syrup

Stir the sweet cherries into the cane sugar syrup and allow to stand for a few minutes.

Mint brittle

100g glucose | 100g fondant | 20g mint

Boil the glucose with the fondant until the mixture turns amber. Pour onto a Silpat sheet and allow to cool. Break the cold glucose fondant into pieces and mix well with the mint. Spread this powder onto a Silpat sheet, allow to melt at a high temperature, cool and break into pieces before serving.

To serve

60ml Amareno cherry syrup | Dried cherries, cut into fine strips | Pumpkin seed slivers | Mint leaves

Pour the buttermilk lassi into a suitable dish, then pour over a spiral of Amareno cherry syrup. Place the marinated cherries on top. Garnish with the mint brittle, cherry strips, pumpkin seed slivers and mint leaves.

Cannelloni with mushrooms

Cannelloni

100ml mushroom or truffle juice | 8 flattened spoons Celluzoon | 100g brown mushrooms | 1 shallot | 20g butter | 1 sprig rosemary | 1 sprig thyme | 1tsp tomato paste | Flat-leaf parsley, cut into fine strips | 4 pieces white pasta dough | 4 pieces green pasta dough

Heat the mushroom juice, add the Celluzoon and stir until completely dissolved. Allow to stand for several hours to allow the whipped-in air to escape. Season lightly with salt.
Cut the mushrooms into 5 mm dice, the shallot to brunoise, then sauté both lightly in the butter. Add the rosemary and thyme. Bind the resulting liquid with the tomato paste and season with salt. Pour onto a flat surface.
Bind the mixture with a little of the Celluzoon and mushroom mixture. Now roll out the pasta dough thinly, spoon the mushroom mixture onto the dough, roll up and cook gently in boiling salted water for 3 to 4 minutes.

Concentrated beef broth

2 l beef broth | 400ml veal jus | 200g diced leek, celeriac and carrot | 400g beef, coarsely minced | 1 bay leaf | 1 sprig thyme | 1 sprig rosemary | 2 egg whites, lightly beaten | Dash of soy sauce | A little mushroom brunoise

Pour the veal jus into the beef broth, add the diced vegetables, the minced beef, the herbs, egg white and the mushroom trimmings from the ravioli recipe. Bring to the boil, stirring continuously, skim, and then simmer for about an hour. Strain through a cloth, then season with salt and the soy sauce. Finally, allow the mushroom brunoise to poach in the concentrated beef broth.

To serve Serve the concentrated beef broth, add the ravioli and garnish.

Woodruff punch with berries

100ml sugar syrup 1:1 | 40ml woodruff syrup | 4 flattened spoons Xanthazoon | 200ml white wine | Zest of 1 lime | 30ml Prosecco | 12 raspberries | 4 physalis, each cut into 8 pieces | Blackcurrants | 4 strawberries, each cut into 8 pieces | Sour cream, whisked smooth

Mix the sugar syrup and the woodruff syrup together, bind with Xanthazoon and add the white wine. Season with the lime zest and allow to cool. Just before serving, add the Prosecco. Serve with the berries and small blobs of sour cream.

Parsley brioche with sardine

Parsley brioche

250g egg yolk | 1 bunch flat-leaf parsley | 40ml olive oil | 20g butter | 20g sugar | 8g salt | 160g egg white | 5 flattened spoons Emulzoon | 50g flour

Blend together the parsley leaves with the egg yolk. Add the olive oil, butter, sugar, salt and egg white and whip lightly. Add the flour and Emulzoon, stir in quickly. Fill into a plastic beaker and heat in a microwave oven at 50% of the maximum power. Remove and allow to cool on a rack.

Sardine

2 sardines | 100ml white vinegar | 5 allspice | 1 bay leaf | 1 stalk flat-leaf parsley | 20g sugar | 3g salt | Rapeseed oil

Fillet the sardines, wash and remove the bones. Mix together the white vinegar, ground allspice, bay leaf, flat-leaf parsley, sugar and salt, add the sardines, and allow to marinate for 90 minutes. Then remove from the marinade, cover completely in rapeseed oil and store. Cut into pieces when required.

To serve

Pine nuts, chopped | Dried tomato flakes | Deep-fried flat-leaf parsley | Balsamic vinegar vinaigrette

Break open the brioche, place on a plate with the sardine fillets. Garnish with the pine nuts, tomato flakes and deep-fried flat-leaf parsley. Season lightly with salt and drizzle with balsamic vinegar vinaigrette

AGAZOON
ALGIZOON
CALAZOON
CELLUZOON
EMULZOON
GELLAZOON LOW
GUAR ZOON
IOTAZOON
LOCUZOON
XANTHAZOON

GELLING

Flexible gels, firm gels, fluid or semi-liquid gels, hot ice – gelling is all this and much more. The gelling process can be infinitely varied using the texturizers Agazoon, Gellazoon, Celluzoon and Iotazoon.

Agazoon

Agazoon, basically agar-agar, is a natural product extracted from red algae and seaweed. It is perfectly safe to eat, has a positive effect on the body's cholesterol levels and speeds up digestion when consumed in large quantities. It is tasteless and odourless and is a good alternative to gelatine.

Agazoon does not dissolve in cold water and will only turn to jelly after having been heated to a temperature above 80 °C. Gelling is fast, and by the time the mass has reached room temperature it can already be cut. This makes it an ideal product for creating all kinds of forms. The jelly can then be heated to 85 °C without its losing its form. Acids reduce the Agazoon's gelling properties.

Celluzoon

Celluzoon, actually cellulose, is made from plant fibers. It is a basically indigestible dietary fiber that is completely safe to use. Celluzoon is easily dissolved in hot water but should always be mixed first into cold water and then brought to the boil in order to achieve the best results. When a mixture containing Celluzoon is heated beyond 60 °C, the resulting jelly is first quite firm and then melts when it cools. This property is used to good effect when creating "hot ice cream", which then "melts" in the mouth.

Celluzoon tolerates high salt and acid concentrations.

Gellazoon

Gellazoon is a gelling agent made of gellan gum. It is a dietary fiber, is completely safe and presents no health hazard. It can, however, speed up digestion.

Only very small quantities of Gellazoon are needed. The gel formed after a mixture containing Gellazoon has been heated and then cooled is clear, has a strong colour and good aroma. However, the gelling properties are less stable in combination with concentrated salt or acidic solutions.

Jellies made only with Gellazoon are inelastic and brittle: using Gellazoon in combination with Agazoon and Locuzoon will overcome this.

Stirring the jelly with a hand blender will create a fluid or semi-liquid gel which will, however, settle back to its jelly state after a while.

Iotazoon

Iotazoon is a gelling and thickening agent derived from carrageen, a polysaccharide extracted from red seaweed. It is an acknowledged food additive with no maximum permissible quantity restrictions.

When Iotazoon is heated and then cooled it turns into a clear jelly: its elasticity depends on the amount of Iotazoon used. When Iotazoon is mixed with liquids containing calcium, the resulting jelly is at the same time flexible and firm. This may not be heat-stable but it can be frozen and then thawed. Calcium, naturally contained in milk products, can be added in the form of Calazoon. Iotazoon reacts to salt and acidity. Gels made with Iotazoon liquefy when shaken or stirred, or even chewed, but return to their gel state when left standing. The food thus, literally, melts in the mouth.

Carrot sheet

Firm jellies made with Agazoon can be heated to 85 °C without them losing their shape. This means that they can be incorporated into warm fillings. A cream cheese filling in a carrot sheet is really delightful.

1

Pour 200ml carrot juice into a Thermomix.

2

Add 5 flattened spoons Agazoon, mix well and heat to at least 80 °C.

3

Pour onto a warmed platter.

4

Spread the mixture evenly over the surface and allow to cool.

5

A carrot sheet cut into strips.

Vinegar pasta

Vinegar pasta is made with Gellazoon. Jellies made with Gellazoon have strong colours and flavours, they are easy to cut and can even be grated.

1

Pour 200ml veal stock and 40ml balsamic vinegar into a Thermomix.

2

Add 14 flattened spoons Gellazoon, mix well and bring to the boil.

3

Pour the mixture into a form and allow to stand until the gel forms.

4

There you have vinegar pasta.

5

Grated vinegar pasta.

Hot orange ice cream

Your guests will be totally surprised when the firm and hot “ice cream” slowly cools in the mouth and then melts!

1

Mix together 200ml orange juice, a dash of orange liqueur, and 1tbsp honey. Add 6 flattened spoons Celluzoon.

2

Blend well with a hand blender and allow to rest for at least 8 hours to allow the whipped-in air to escape.

3

Pour the orange mixture into half-moon shaped dishes and allow to set in an oven at 120 °C.

4

Tip the orange “ice cream” out of its form and serve.

Passion fruit gum

A mass bound with Iotazoon is heated and then cooled again to form a clear jelly. When it is now shaken or stirred, or later chewed, it turns back into a liquid. A really sumptuous feeling in the mouth!

1

Pour 100ml passion fruit juice and 40g sugar into a Thermomix.

2

Add 6 flattened spoons Iotazoon, mix and heat to at least 80 °C.

3

Pour the passion fruit mixture into a dish and allow to cool.

4

Tip the passion fruit gum out of its form and serve.

Herbed blini with caviar

Herb blini

100ml parsley water | 8 flattened spoons Celluzoon | Fleur de Sel | 100ml rapeseed oil

Whisk the Celluzoon into the parsley water and cool down to 4 °C, so that the two bind well. Season this solution with salt and stir lightly in a food processor. With the machine running, pour in the rapeseed oil slowly, as if making mayonnaise. Pour the mixture into a small iSi siphon and screw on a charger. Put small metal rings onto a non-stick baking tray, add the blini mixture with the siphon and bake for 2 minutes at 180 °C. Remove from the tray and serve.

Crème fraîche quenelles

40g crème fraîche | Fleur de Sel | White vinegar | Toasted pain d'épice

Whip the Fleur de Sel and the vinegar together. Form small quenelles with two warmed spoons and serve on the toasted pain d'épice with the herb blini.

To serve

40g trout caviar | Chervil | Deep-dried sage leaves | Onion sprouts | Estragon leaves, finely cut

Place the blinis on a plate, top with the caviar, chervil and sage. Garnish with the crème fraîche quenelles, the onion sprouts and estragon.

Malt beer jelly with liver paté

Malt beer jelly

200ml malt beer | 5 flattened spoons Agazoon | Balsamic vinegar

Whisk the Agazoon into the malt beer and boil up once. Pour half of the mixture into a flat, rectangular dish and allow to get cold. Allow the rest to cool a little, then add the balsamic vinegar. Now whisk this until fluffy, pour into a second rectangular dish and put in the fridge to set: the foam will set immediately.

Liver paté

200g duck liver | 1 shallot, finely diced | 1 apple, finely diced | 1 twig rosemary | 2 juniper berries | 1 allspice berry, ground | 50ml port | 20ml sherry | 100ml chicken stock | 3 leaves gelatine | 100ml whipped cream

Lightly sauté the duck liver with the shallot and the apple. Add the rosemary and spices. Deglaze with the port and sherry. Allow to cool, remove the spices, add the chicken stock, mix well and then pass through a fine sieve. Dissolve the soaked gelatine and mix into the liver mixture. Allow to stand until slightly firm, then add the whipped cream. Pour into a rectangular dish and put into the fridge.

To serve

Diced artichoke, sautéed in olive oil | Diced tomato | Balsamic vinegar vinaigrette | Deep-fried strips of artichoke | Thyme

Cut the liver paté into slices. Marinate the diced artichoke and tomato in the vinaigrette, then place on the paté. Top with the deep-fried strips of artichoke, thyme and the finely-diced malt beer jelly. Garnish with a slice of malt beer jelly.

Raspberry gum with mint pesto

Raspberry gum

100ml raspberry juice | 10ml raspberry vinegar | 6 flattened spoons Iotazoon | 40g sugar | 2g ascorbic acid

Mix the raspberry juice with the vinegar and whisk in the Iotazoon. Bring to the boil once. Fill into individual Silpat forms and refrigerate. Mix the sugar and ascorbic acid together. Coat the raspberry gums in this mixture.

Mint pesto

1 bunch mint | 40ml sugar syrup 1:1 | 20ml olive oil | 20ml rapeseed oil | 30g almonds | Zest of 1 lime

Mix all the ingredients into a homogenous mass in a Thermomix. Store in a preserving jar with a rubber seal. Use as required.

To serve

100g raspberries | 20ml lime oil | Mint leaves | 20g Muscovado sugar

Draw a design on a plate with the mint pesto. Set the raspberry gum in the middle, surround with the raspberries and garnish with the mint leaves. Sprinkle with Muscavdo sugar.

Parsley pavé with flowers

Parsley pavé

400ml parsley water | 10 flattened spoons Agazoon | Fleur de Sel | 10ml white vinegar | Pinch of sugar

Mix everything together and bring to the boil once. Skim, pour into a flat dish and allow to cool. Cut as required and serve.

Flowers and vinaigrette

50g various edible flowers | 50g sunflower sprouts | 1tsp shallot vinegar | 1tsp fish stock | 1tsp rapeseed oil

Prepare the flowers and the sunflower sprouts. Make a vinaigrette with the shallot vinegar, fish stock and rapeseed oil, season with a little salt.

To serve

1 brioche | Tasmanian pepper | Parsley purée

Place the pave on a plate, arrange the flowers and sprouts on top, sprinkle with the vinaigrette. Break the brioche into tiny pieces, fry lightly and place on top. Sprinkle with the pepper. Serve with a little parsley purée on the side.

Pea dumplings with langoustine

Pea dumplings 10 flattened spoons Celluzoon | 100ml water | 50g peas | Mint julienne

Dissolve the Celluzoon in warm water, then leave in the fridge for several hours to allow the whipped-in air to escape. Season with a little salt. Mix the peas with the mint. Add enough Celluzoon solution to completely cover the peas. Form little quenelles with the pea mixture and put onto a tray. Poach in salted water at 80 °C as required.

Langoustine 4 langoustines | Olive oil | 20ml Noilly Prat | 1 dash lime juice | Maldon sea salt

Break open the langoustines, remove the black vein and marinate in a mixture of Noilly Prat and olive oil. Then season with lime juice and Maldon sea salt. Heat through in an oven at 180 °C for 2 minutes, then pat dry.

Bacon powder 100g rye bread | 100g fat bacon (fat only), fried and dried | Salt | Lime zest

Put all the ingredients into a grinder and grind very finely. Store in a screw-top jar and use as required.

To serve Green pea purée with cream

Place the green pea purée on a plate, with a pea dumpling on top. Lay the langoustine over both and season with a little salt. Sprinkle with bacon powder and garnish with a little mint.

Pineapple with tea pasta

Tea pasta 250ml green tea | 10 flattened spoons Gellazoon | 1tbsp honey

Mix all the ingredients together and boil up once. Skim, pour into a tall container and allow to get cold. Take out of the container and either shave off a portion with a vegetable slicer or grate with a fine Microplan grater.

Pineapple 1 pineapple | 50g pineapple purée | Pepper

Cut the main part of the pineapple into oblong pieces, and dice the trimmings. Bind with the pineapple purée and sweeten if necessary. Season with a little pepper.

Milk foam 150ml low-fat milk | 30g vanilla sugar | 3 flattened spoons Emulzoon

Heat the milk to 50 °C and whisk in the remaining ingredients, making sure to incorporate plenty of air. Allow the milk froth to stand for one minute.

To serve 20g dried barberry berries | Pinch saffron powder | Shiso cress

Soak the dried barberry berries in warm water and allow to drain well. Season with saffron. Place the pineapple purée on a plate. Grill the oblong pineapple pieces and place on top. Lay the tea pasta slices on top and garnish with barberry berries and cress. Serve a little of the stable milk foam on the side.

PUMKIN SEED PASTA

Pumpkin seed spaghetti with porcini essence

Pumpkin mixture

1 bunch flat-leaf parsley | 200ml water | 20 flattened spoons Celluzoon | Pinch Fleur de Sel | 50ml rapeseed oil | 50ml pumpkin seed oil

Mix the parsley in a blender with the water until very fine. Allow to stand until the foam has subsided, then continue to mix, add the Celluzoon, a little salt and the oils. This is best made the day before it is needed to allow the whipped-in air to escape.

Porcini essence

500ml beef broth | 200ml veal jus | 70g diced mixed leek, celeriac and carrot | 100g beef, coarsely minced | 150g porcini | 1 egg white, lightly beaten | 1 sprig rosemary | 1 sprig thyme | 1tbsp soy sauce | 6tbsp diced porcini

Pour the veal jus into the beef broth, then add the diced vegetables, minced beef, porcini, egg white and herbs. Bring to the boil, stirring continuously, skim, and then simmer for about an hour. Strain through a cloth, then season with salt and the soy sauce. Finally, allow the diced porcini to poach in the concentrated beef broth.

To serve

Toasted bread with porcini duxelles

Draw the pumpkin seed mixture into syringes or squeeze bottles and serve with the very hot porcini essence, so that each guest can make their own spaghetti in the hot soup. Serve with toasted bread and porcini duxelles.

Basil jelly with cream cheese

Basil jelly

200ml parsley water | 1 bunch basil | 5 flattened spoons Agazoon | Fleur de Sel | Tomato vinegar

Put the parsley water and basil leaves into a blender and pulse until fine, then pass through a sieve. Season with Fleur de Sel and tomato vinegar. Whisk in the Agazoon and boil up once. Pour onto a warmed platter and, when cold, store in a fridge.

Cream cheese

200g cream cheese | 20g crème fraîche | 1 leaf gelatine | 2tbsp olive oil | White balsamic vinegar | 2tbsp whipped cream | 1 slice gingerbread

Whisk the crème cheese into the crème fraîche. Dissolve the softened gelatine in the warmed olive oil, then add this mixture to the cream cheese. Season with salt and balsamic vinegar. Fold in the whipped cream. Pour into a rectangular dish and allow to set. Fry the crumbled gingerbread.

To serve

Basil cress | Thin radish slices | Society garlic

Cut the cream cheese into slices and wrap in a basil sheet. Put on a plate with the toasted gingerbread crumbs and the radish slices. Garnish with the flowers and leaves of the society garlic.

AGAZOON
ALGIZOON
CALAZOON
CELLUZOON
EMULZOON
GELLAZOON LOW
GUAR ZOON
IOTAZOON
LOCUZOON
XANTHAZOON

THICKENERS

Viscose textures, emulsifying properties, floating herbs, creamy mouth feel – thickeners can be all these and more. To achieve a particular effect just choose a suitable additive, put your specialist knowledge to good use and, hey presto! Truly fantastic results.

Guarzoon

Guarzoon contains guar gum which is extracted from the seeds of the guar bean. It is totally safe. It is used mainly as a thickener and stabiliser, giving liquids a high viscosity; this makes them behave both like a liquid and a gel. Guarzoon may not form firm jellies, but it can be easily dissolved, is stable in both a frozen state and when thawing, and is a good emulsifier, a property which can be used to stabilise foams. A combination of Guarzoon and Xanthazoon is to be recommended if strong, elastic jellies are required.

Guarzoon is used in many ways in molecular cuisine. As it works well with acids it is often used to create viscose sauces from wine or vinegar reductions with fine particles suspended in them. Stable foams are created with the help of a siphon. Guarzoon is also widely used to create ice cream, parfait or sorbets as it delays the growth of ice crystals, creating a better mouth feel. The degree of viscosity is determined by the dose.

Xanthazoon

Xanthazoon contains xanthan, a natural thickening and stabilizing agent. It is made by a fermentation process involving a special bacteria and sucrose products such as cornmeal, is entirely natural and is an acknowledged safe food additive.

Xanthazoon dissolves in both hot and cold liquids and, thanks to its tremendous ability to swell and at the same time thicken, turns these liquids into fluid jellies. The viscous property of the emulsified liquid remains even when heated; the dose determines the density. Xanthazoon's emulsifying properties are what make it so special, viscose products have a better mouth feel and it work with acid. Xanthazoon works well to create culinary emulsions such as dressings, sauce or even drinks, and allows small particles to be held in suspension. A hand blender is the best tool to mix the powder with a liquid. Another recommendation is to start from a basic solution made with water.

Locuzoon

Locuzoon contains locust bean gum, which is extracted from the seeds of the carob tree growing in Mediterranean countries. It is a totally safe dietary fiber that even lowers cholesterol levels. Locuzoon is particularly easy to dissolve in hot liquids: when cold it creates a viscose texture that can also be heat-stable, depending on the dose. It can, however, also be mixed with a little cold liquid and then stirred into hot liquids.

Locuzoon works with acids and tolerates high salt concentrations. It also delays the growth of ice crystals in jellies giving frozen products a nice mouth feel.

The use of Locuzoon and Xanthazoon together are recommended if strong, elastic textures are required.

Locuzoon

Locuzoon is used to thicken sauces with a high salt or acid concentration.

1

200ml vegetable stock mixed with 100ml vinegar.

2

Add 4 flattened spoons Locuzoon.

3

Whisk together with a hand blender.

4

The sauce is finished.

Apple mousse

Using a mixture of Guarzoon and Xanthazoon makes this apple mousse really creamy and stable.

1

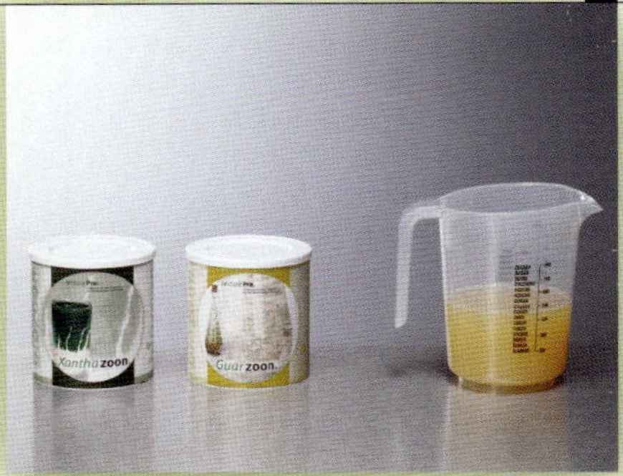

Measure 350ml apple juice.

2

Add 1 flattened spoon Guarzoon and 2 flattened spoons Xanthazoon.

3

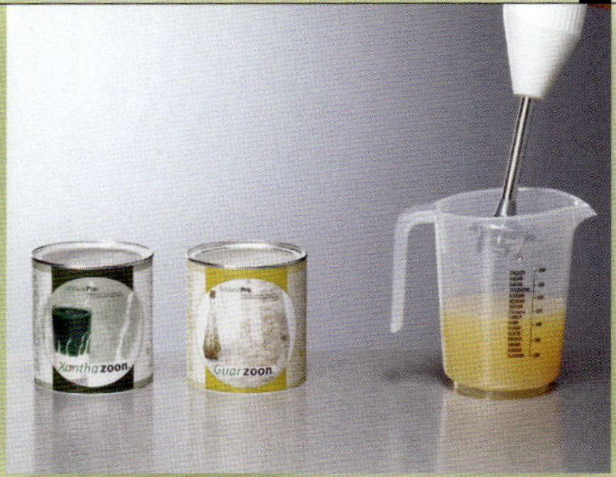

Whisk with a hand blender.

4

Fill the mixture into a 0.5 litre iSi siphon, screw on a charger and keep in the fridge until required.

5

Spray the apple mousse into a dish.

6

There is the finished apple mousse.

Clear vanilla sauce with wild peach

Clear vanilla sauce

100ml sugar syrup 2:1 | 1 vanilla pod | Few drops lemon juice | 1 flattened spoon Xanthazoon

Whisk the sugar syrup together with the other ingredients carefully and stand in the fridge. Vacuum seal if necessary to get rid of any remaining air bubbles.

Wild peach

2 wild peaches | 50g butter | 10g sugar

Remove the stone from the peach. Cut into eight thin segments. Glaze in the butter and sugar.

Cocoa ice cream

120g egg yolk (6 egg yolks) | 80g sugar | 500g cream | 30g cocoa powder | 80g dark chocolate | Juice of 1 lime | 1 flattened spoon Xanthazoon

Whisk the egg yolks and sugar together. Bring the milk and cocoa to the boil, add the chocolate. Pour this cocoa mass onto the egg yolk mixture, whisking all the time. Return to the pan and stir gently over a low heat until thickened. Add lime juice to taste and allow to cool. Whisk in the Xanthazoon. Pour the mixture into a Paco Jet and freeze for at least 24 hours. Shave off portions as required.

To serve

Toasted brioche | Mint | Mint sprigs, deep-fried and coated in sugar

Place a portion of the clear vanilla sauce on a plate, top with the peach segments and place a warm brioche on the side. Garnish with the mint and serve.

Vinegar coulis with marinated olives

Vinegar coulis 4 flattened spoons Locuzoon | 200ml vegetable stock | 100ml vinegar | 1 sprig each rosemary and thyme

Whisk the Locuzoon, stock and vinegar together and boil up once. Pour into a jug, add the herbs and season lightly with salt. Use as required.

Maple syrup cucumbers 30ml balsamic vinegar | 2tbsp maple syrup | 4 pieces of cucumber (2cm x 2cm), seeds removed | 1/2 flattened spoon Locuzoon

Mix the vinegar with the maple syrup, thicken with Locuzoon. Pour into the lightly salted cucumber pieces.

To serve 40g black olives, in strips | 40g cucumber, diced | 10 tomato flakes | Shiso cress | 20ml vinaigrette with white balsamic vinegar

Place the cucumbers filled with maple syrup on a plate. Season the vinegar coulis and draw a decorative design round the cucumber. Marinate the olives and cucumber in the vinaigrette, season lightly with salt. Add to the plate, and garnish with tomato flakes and cress.

Frankfurt herbs with char

Frankfurt herbs 200ml fish stock | 100g mixed herbs (borage, chervil, cress, parsley, salad burnet, sorrel, chives) | Few drops vinegar | Fleur de Sel | 2 flattened spoons Xanthazoon

Mix all the ingredients in a Thermomix. Whisk in the Xanthazoon and season. The char fillets can be glazed with the Frankfurt herb mixture.

Char 4 char fillets á 60g, prepared | 20ml lime oil

Drizzle the char fillets with the lime oil and bake in an oven for 12 minutes at 50 °C. Season lightly with salt. Allow to cool to room temperature before serving.

To serve Iced soured potato purée | Glazed fennel with fennel green | Fried onions | Skin of the char, baked between sheets of baking paper | Balsamic vinegar vinaigrette

To make the potato purée, purée one day old cooked potatoes with sour cream, season with salt and pepper. Place a portion of the purée on the glazed fennel, garnish with fennel green. Place the char fillet on the potato purée, top with a potato purée quenelle and season with a little pepper. Garnish with the baked skin and the fried onions. Drizzle with a little vinaigrette.

Salmon with orange marinade

Salmon

4 salmon fillets á 40g | 30ml lime oil

Drizzle the salmon fillets with the lime oil and bake in an oven for 18 minutes at 50 °C. Allow to cool.

Orange marinade

200ml orange juice, slightly reduced | 12 flattened spoons Locuzoon | 3g salt | 20ml olive oil

Whisk all the ingredients together and boil up once. Pour over the salmon whisIt still hot and allow to marinade for 4 hours.

To serve

24 spears Thai asparagus, blanched | 40g orange segments prepared in nitrogen (see page 136, "Lime fillets with Mojito air") | 40ml orange vinaigrette | Onion seeds | Maldon sea salt

Marinade the asparagus in the orange vinaigrette, then place on a plate. Slice the salmon and add to the plate. Garnish with the orange fillets, drizzle with vinaigrette. Sprinkle with the onion seeds and a little Maldon Sea Salt.

Vegetable stew with olive oil

Vegetable stew

300ml vegetable stock | 3 flattened spoons Guarzoon | 1 star anise | 1 mace | 5 peppercorns, ground | A few drops soya sauce

Whisk Guarzoon into the vegetable stock and boil up once. Put the spices into a little bag, hang into the broth and poach. Season with soya sauce and a little salt.

1 Romanesco broccoli | 1 kohlrabi | 1 bunch carrots with green | 1 small packet baby corn | 1 bunch spring onions

Cut the vegetables into even-sized pieces and blanch in salt water (14g salt per litre). Cool quickly in iced water. Warm through in the broth as required.

To serve

30ml olive oil

Glaze the vegetables individually in the broth before serving. Dribble a little olive oil over the broth before serving.

Herby mayonnaise with poached egg

Herby mayonnaise

50ml vegetable stock | 30g salad burnet | 30g flat-leaf parsley | 30g chervil | 2 flattened spoons Guarzoon | a little mustard | Few drops lemon juice | Fleur de Sel | 150ml rapeseed oil

Blend the vegetable stock and the herbs in a Thermo Mix and thicken with Guarzoon. Add the mustard, lemon juice and salt. With the mixer on, add the oil in a thin stream. Season well. Store in a preserving jar.

Poached eggs

4 eggs | 80ml vinegar | Fleur de Sel

Heat a pan of water to 60 °C. Break each egg into a ladle with 20ml vinegar, stir a vortex in the water with the ladle and allow each egg to glide into th s vortex. Poach gently for 4 minutes, then remove with a slotted spoon. Reheat under a salamander before serving, adding a little salt.

To serve

30g chervil | 10g estragon | 30g Shiso cress | 30g chicory leaves | Apple vinaigrette

Mix the herbs and chicory leaves to create a salad, marinate with the apple vinaigrette. Place the herby mayonnaise on a plate, top with an egg. Place the salad on the side and perhaps sprinkle with a few toasted croutons.

AGAZOON
ALGIZOON
CALAZOON
CELLUZOON
EMULZOON
GELLAZOON LOW
GUAR ZOON
IOTAZOON
LOCUZOON
XANTHAZOON

COMBINED AGENTS

MANY OF THE "TEXTUREPRO" TEXTURIZERS CAN BE COMBINED WITHOUT ANY PROBLEMS WHATSOEVER, SOMETIMES ENTIRELY NEW PROPERTIES ARE CREATED WITH EXCITING APPLICATIONS. THE WORD "COMBINE" IS THE KEY WORD TO MOVING INTO A WHOLE NEW WORLD OF MOLECULAR CUISINE.

Pistachio sheet with corn-fed chicken

Pistachio sheet

200ml chicken stock | 6 flattened spoons Agazoon | Fleur de Sel | 20g pistachios, finely chopped

Whisk the chicken stock and Agazoon together and boil up once. Season well, then stir in the pistachios. Pour onto a pre-heated plastic tray in a thin layer and allow to cool. Cut into broad strips when required.

Corn-fed chicken

4 corn-fed chicken breasts | 4 sprigs rosemary | 4 wide strips of orange zest

Remove skin from the chicken breasts, place between two Silpat sheets and roast in the oven at 160 °C. Place the chicken breast, rosemary and orange zest in a plastic vacuum pouch and vacuum seal. Cook in a water bath for 30 minutes at 56 °C. Fry in foaming butter and season lightly with salt. Keep warm until required, then cut into slices.

To serve

Tandoori paste | 8 potato dice | 2g saffron threads | Pea sprouts | Chicken jus reduction

Draw a decorative line across the plate with the Tandoori paste. Place the chicken breast on the line, top with the pistachio sheet and roast chicken skin. Place a potato dice at the end of each line and season with salt. Sprinkle with saffron threads and pea sprouts. Serve the chicken jus reduction extra.

Hot orange ice cream with Campari caviar

Orange ice cream

200ml orange juice | Zest of 1/4 orange | Dash Grand Manier | 1tbsp honey | 6 flattened spoons Celluzoon

Mix all the ingredients together with a hand blender to make a homogenous mass. Allow to rest for at least 8 hours. Fill into forms when required and bake at 120 °C.

Campari caviar

20g basil seeds | 100ml cold water | 20ml Campari | 1tsp honey a little lemon zest and juice

Soak the basil seeds for about one minute in water. Allow to drain on a sieve. Marinate with Campari immediately and season with the remaining ingredients.

To serve

Orange fillets | Mint leaf tips | Orange zest

Place the orange fillets on a plate, top with the Campari caviar and place a scoop of hot orange ice cream on the side. Garnish with the mint and orange zest.

Froth with oxtail

Froth with oxtail

Oxtail 6 large pieces of oxtail | 100g mirepoix | 1 piece bacon rind | 1 clove garlic | 1tbsp tomato paste | 20ml soy sauce | 20ml balsamic vinegar | 200ml full-bodied red wine | 1 bouquet garni (rosemary, thyme, flat-leaf parsley, bay leaf) | Pepper and allspice, freshly ground | 500ml veal stock | 30g Celluzoon solution

Fry the oxtail well on all sides in hot oil, season lightly with salt, then remove from the pan. Add the mirepoix, bacon rind and garlic, then the tomato paste and fry. Deglaze with the soy sauce, balsamic vinegar and red wine. Reduce this liquid until only a very little is left. Add the bouquet garni, allspice, pepper and veal stock. Bring to the boil and skim. Put into a plastic vacuum pouches with the oxtail and cook for 36 hours in a Julabo water bath at 72 °C. Pull the meat off the bones. Mix the Celluzoon solution into the warm oxtail meat and weight down. Store in the fridge.

Froth

100g shin of beef, coarsely chopped | 30g chopped vegetables (celeriac, leek, carrot) | 1 small bouquet garni (see above) | 1 small onion, fried until golden | 4 flattened spoons Xanthazoon | 2 flattened spoons Guarzoon

Strain the oxtail stock, then clarify with the shin of beef, vegetables, bouquet garni and onion. Allow to simmer for one hour, then strain. There should be 700ml consommé left. Whisk the Xanthazoon and Guarzoon into the cold stock, season and pour into an espuma bottle. Screw on a charger immediately and allow to stand in the fridge for at least 4 hours. Screw on a second charger if required.

To serve

Knaki pastry, fried in butter | Celery, cut into diamonds and blanched | King trumpet mushrooms, sautéd in butter | 40ml reduced veal stock

Cut the oxtail into suitably-sized pieces and place between the sheets of kanaki pastry. Heat through quickly. Serve with the celery and mushrooms. Fill the froth into a glass and complete with jus.

Cherries in aspic with cream

Cherries in aspic

100ml cherry juice | 50ml port | 4 flattened spoons Agazoon | Zest of 1/2 a lime | 12 cherries | 10g marzipan flavoured with Kirsch schnaps

Whisk together the juice, port, lime zest and bring to the boil once. Remove the stones from 4 cherries from the underside and stuff with marzipan. Put in the fridge. Remove the stones from the remaining cherries and cut in half. Put four halves aside, then quarter the rest.
Allow the cherry stock to cool a little. Dip the stuffed cherries into the cooling liquid to glaze. Glaze the cherry halves in the same way. Pour the stock over the cherries in a form and allow to set in the fridge.

Cream

40g crème fraîche | 15 sugar

Stir together well and keep in the fridge.

Cherry stock

50ml cherry stock | 1/2 flattened spoon Xanthazoon

Whisk the Xanthazoon into the stock and vacuum seal.

To serve

Baked rolled filo pastry | Tasmanian pepper | Mint leaf tips

Remove the cherries from the form, cut into pieces as required and serve surrounded by the other cherries. Sprinkle with pepper and filo pastry. Spoon the cream onto the plate and serve with cherry stock and mint tips.

Veal stock cannelloni with vegetables

Veal stock cannelloni

200ml concentrated veal stock with very little salt | 16 flattened spoons Gellazoon

Whisk the Gellazoon into the stock and bring to the boil once. Pour onto a pre-heated plastic tray in a thin layer and allow to cool. Cut into squares and then roll up into tubes using a metal rod. Press down a little to seal the edges and pull from the rod.

Veal stock

200ml veal stock | 1 flattened spoons Guarzoon | 10ml soy sauce | 1 clove garlic

Whisk the Guarzoon into the veal stock and bring to the boil once. Season with soy sauce, poaching the lightly squashed garlic in the mass.

To serve

30g leek julienne | 30g carrot julienne | Flat-leaf parsley

Serve the cannelloni with the vegetables and garnish with the parsley. Spoon the stock over the dish just before serving.

Vinegar roly-poly

Roly-poly 200ml vegetable stock | 16 flattened spoons Gellazoon | 20ml soy sauce

Whisk the Gellazoon into the stock and bring to the boil once. Season with soy sauce and pour onto a pre-heated plastic tray in a thin layer and allow to cool. Cut into rectangles.

Salad Wild herb salad with flowers | Elder flower vinaigrette

Pull the salad leaves into small pieces and marinate with the vinaigrette.

To serve Balsamic vinegar in an atomizer | Potato straw | Vinegar sauce | Candied olive pieces

Spray the sheet lightly with the vinegar, top with a portion of salad, season with salt and roll up tightly. Cut into even-sized pieces and serve. Garnish with vinegar sauce, potato straw. Sprinkle with olives.

Gazpacho with texturizers

Gazpacho with texturizers

Gazpacho

2 cucumbers | 6 bell peppers | 500g tomato juice | 100g toasted almonds | 100ml olive oil | Young garlic | Red wine vinegar | Salt, pepper, sugar, chilli oil | 6 flattened spoons Xanthazoon

Prepare the vegetables. Purée in a ThermoMix together with all the other ingredients and season well. Pass through a fine sieve and fill into an espuma bottle. There should be 900ml liquid. Put into the fridge.

Hot bell pepper jelly

400ml bell pepper juice | 12 flattened spoons Agazoon | Red wine vinegar | Salt and pepper

Mix all the ingredients together cold, season well, then bring to the boil once. Skim off, pour into a dish and allow to get cold. Cut into equally sized pieces and heat in an oven at 90 °C when required.

Cucumber ravioli

200ml cucumber water made from fresh cucumbers | 3 flattened spoons Algizoon | Salt, pepper, chilli oil | Calazoon bath

Whisk the Algizoon into the cucumber water and season well. Vacuum seal to get rid of all the air bubbles. Using a dosage spoon, create spheres of the mixture in a Calazoon bath and cook for 2 minutes. Remove and rinse in salt water.

To serve Garlic crisps | Toasted pine nuts | Creamed white onions | Olive oil | Fried onions and onion seeds | Society garlic

Place a piece of hot bell pepper jelly on a plate and garnish with garlic crisps and pine nuts. Fill the gazpacho into an iSi siphon, screw on two chargers, shake well and spray onto a dish. Add the creamed onion to the plate and drizzle with olive oil. Place the gazpacho and the ravioli on a plate, garnish with fried onions, onion seeds and society garlic.

Effervescent sangria melon

Sangria

600ml red wine | 20ml Cointreau | 20ml Spanish brandy | 100g sugar | 2 organic oranges | 1 organic lemon

Grate the zest of the orange and lemon, then cut the fruit into slices. Mix all the liquid ingredients together, add the fruit and zest allow to marinate overnight. Strain the sangria before using.

Melon

400ml sangria | 20 flattened spoons Gellazoon | 1 cavaillon melon | Endive leaves

Wisk the Gellazoon into the sangria and boil up once. Pour onto warmed Silpat mats and put in the fridge to get cold. Cut the melon into pieces, wrap in the sangria sheets and cut into suitably-sized pieces. Serve on a spoon garnished with an endive leaf.

To serve

350ml sangria | 2 flattened spoons Xanthazoon | 1 flattened spoon Guarzoon

Wisk the texturizers into the sangria, fill into a 0.5 litre iSi siphon and screw on two chargers. Spray the sangria into a glass dish, and lay the spoon with the sangria melon on it across the top.

Wheat espuma with banana compote

Banana compote

200ml banana juice | 50g banana, diced | 3 flattened spoons Iotazoon | 1 vanilla pod

Whisk the Iotazoon into the banana juice and boil up once. Add the seeds of the vanilla pod and the diced banana. Fill into glass dishes and put in the fridge.

Wheat espuma

50ml sugar syrup 1:1 | 300ml wheat beer | 2 flattened spoons Xanthazoon | 1 flattened spoon Guarzoon

Mix the sugar syrup and wheat beer together, then whisk into the texturizers. Pour into a 0.5 litre siphon, screw on a charger and store in the fridge.

To serve

4 slices caramelised banana | Shiso cress

Spray the wheat espuma onto the banana compote. Skewer the caramelised banana slices, garnish with the cress and place across the glass dish.

Veal jus with trout

Veal jus

250ml veal jus, without thickener | 30g brown butter | 1 flattened spoon Xanthazoon

Bring the veal jus to the boil with the butter, whisk in the Xanthazoon and allow the air bubbles to escape.

Trout

4 trout fillets | A little tempura flour | 40ml rapeseed oil | 20ml olive oil | 1 sprig rosemary | 8 lime fillets

Dust the trout fillets with the tempura flour. Fry in the rapeseed oil, skin side down. Transfer to an oven and bake for a further 3 minutes at 150 °C, also skin side down. Remove and pat dry with kitchen paper. Season with a little salt. Add the rosemary to the olive oil, heat to 50 °C and add the lime fillets to warm them. Serve on the trout fillet.

To serve

Potato brunoise | Olive oil | Radish slivers | Marjoram leaves

Fry the diced potatoes in the olive oil until crisp and brown. Place the trout fillet onto a plate, pour the veal jus onto the plate. Lay the diced potatoes on the trout. Garnish with radish slivers and marjoram.

Mojito with texturizers

Mojito with texturizers

Base mixture

1100ml Bitter Lemon | 8 limes | 1 bunch mint | 230ml brown rum | 220g brown sugar

Crush and mix all the ingredients together. Keep overnight in the fridge.

As gel

200ml base mixture | 6 flattened spoons Gellazoon | Zest of 1 lime

Whisk the Gellazoon into the base mixture and boil up once. Pour into a glass jar and put in the fridge. To serve, cut into thin slices and garnish with lime zest.

As espuma

350ml base mixture | 2 flattened spoons Guarzoon | 2 flattened spoons Xanthazoon

Whisk everything together. Pour into a 0.5 litre iSi siphon and screw on a charger.

As sphere

200ml base mixture | 25g Algizoon mixture | Calazoon bath | Mint

Mix the base Mojito mixture and the Algizoon mixture together carefully. Dip this new mixture into a Calazoon bath with a dosing spoon to form spheres. Rinse in either water or Bitter Lemon. Garnish with mint.

Lime fillets with Mojito air

1 lime | Liquid nitrogen | 7 flattened spoons Emulzoon | 400ml base mixture

Cut the lime into fillets and dip these in the liquid nitrogen. Press between two layers of baking paper, then store in the freezer until required. Whisk the Emulzoon into the base mixture in a large bowl. Allow the mixture to stabilise for one minute, then remove with a slotted spoon and place on the lime fillets that have been dusted with sugar. Serve immediately.

Caramel ice cream with apricots

Caramel ice cream

100g sugar | 350ml milk | 250ml cream | 1tbsp glucose | 1/2 vanilla pod | 8 egg yolks | 1 flattened spoon Xanthazoon | 200g crème fraîche

Put half the sugar in a saucepan and cook gently until nice and brown. Dissolve the caramel with the milk, then add the cream, glucose and vanilla seeds, bring to the boil and simmer for a few moments. Whisk the egg yolks with the remaining sugar, then pour on the vanilla milk and simmer until the consistency of thin cream. Now whisk in the Xanthazoon and fold in the crème fraîche. Pour into an ice machine and allow to freeze.

Apricots

2 apricots | 30ml white wine | 30g honey | A few drops of lemon juice

Remove the stones from the apricots and quarter them. Bring the white wine, honey and lemon juice to the boil, add the apricots and allow to poach until lightly glazed and marinated.

To serve

Umeboshi paste | Mint brittle | Mint leaves

Scoop a quenelle of ice cream onto a plate. Draw a thin line Umeboshi paste across the ice cream. Add the apricot with its liquor. Garnish with mint brittle and mint leaves.

Suckling pig with cucumber yoghurt

Suckling pig with cucumber yoghurt

Suckling pig

1 loin of suckling pig, with bone | 3g caraway seeds | 3g mustard seeds | Fleur de Sel | 30ml olive oil

Prepare the loin of suckling pig, place in a plastic vacuum pouch with the remaining ingredients and vacuum seal. Cook in a Julabo water bath for 25 minutes at 58 °C. Then fry on the skin side until crisp.

1 piece belly of suckling pig | 200ml veal stock | 30ml malt beer | 1tsp mustard | 1 sprig rosemary | 1 flattened spoon Xanthazoon

Prepare the belly of suckling pig, sear in a hot pan. When cool place in a plastic vacuum pouch with the stock, beer, mustard and rosemary and vacuum seal. Cook in a Julabo water bath for 60 minutes at 62 °C. Remove from the pouch and reduce the liquor a little. Thicken with Xanthazoon and season well. Glaze the belly with this liquor.

Cucumber yoghurt

200g yoghurt | 1 flattened spoon Guarzoon | A few drops of vinegar

Whisk the Guarzoon into the yoghurt and season with the vinegar and a little salt.

TO SERVE 30G DICED CUCUMBER | 50G DIAMOND-SHAPED CUCUMBER PIECES | 3 COOKED, GLAZED AND BROWNED BORETTANE ONIONS | CUCUMBER AIR (400ML CUCUMBER JUICE AND 7 FLATTENED SPOONS EMULZOON, FOR RECIPE SEE SEITE 136 "MOJITO WITH TEXTURIZERS") | 1 CHARD LEAF

Cut the glazed belly of suckling pig into portions and put onto plates. Now cut slices off the loin, place these on the belly and season with salt. Place the cucumber yoghurt alongside the meat, top with the diced cucumber. Spoon the cucumber diamonds and the Borettane onions alongside. Add some of the liquor from the suckling pig belly. Finally add the cucumber air and garnish with the chard.

Vegetable lentils with wild herb salad

Vegetable lentils

100ml carrot juice | 100ml leek juice | 100ml celeriac juice | 3 flattened spoons Algizoon | 5 flattened spoons Calazoon in 130ml water

Prepare the vegetable lentil mixture one day in advance: stir the Algizoon into the vegetable juice taking care not to incorporate any air bubbles. Season with a little salt. The next day draw the mixture into syringes and dribble into the Calazoon solution. Lift out after 2 minutes and rinse in cold water. The lentils need to be gelled all the way through so that they can be heated.

Vegetable stock

50ml vegetable stock | 1tbsp Argan oil | 1tbsp butter

Heat the vegetable stock, season with Argan oil and thicken with butter. Whisk lightly.

To serve

Wild herb salat | Crackling of suckling pig

Toss the vegetable lentils quickly in butter to heat through. Place in a deep plate with the stock, garnish with the wild herbs and suckling pig crackling.

Ham air with scallops

Ham air with scallops

Ham air

200ml chicken stock | 100g fatty ham | A little salt | 10ml white vinegar | 5 flattened spoons Emulzoon

Heat the chicken stock to 60 °C, add the ham and allow to poach for 1 hour. Strain, then whisk in the other ingredients. Season well, then whisk hard in a large bowl. Allow to stand for one minute, then scoop off the foam.

Scallops

4 scallops | 30ml olive oil | Tempura flour | Maldon Sea Salt | Tasmanian pepper

Dust the scallops with tempura flour. Fry in olive oil for one minute on each side. Keep warm.

Ham jelly

200ml dark chicken stock | 70g pancetta rind | 5 flattened spoons Agazoon | 10ml balsamic vinegar | 1tsp mustard | Chopped pine nuts

Heat the chicken stock to 60 °C, add the pancetta rind and allow to poach for 20 minutes. Strain and whisk in the Agazoon. Season with vinegar and mustard. Bring to the boil once, pour into a glass dish and store in the fridge. Cut into pieces as required and garnish with pine nuts.

To serve 100ml pumpkin juice | 1 flattened spoon Xanthazoon | Ginger caviar (prepare as Campari caviar on page 112, but with ginger juice) | Fried pancetta | Atsina cress

Thicken the pumpkin juice with the Xanthazoon and spoon onto a plate. Top with the jelly. Place the scallop halves on the ginger caviar and top with pancetta. Scoop the ham air onto the plate and garnish with the cress.

Passion fruit sabayon with coral grouper

Passion fruit sabayon

150ml passion fruit purée | 100ml olive oil | 6 flattened spoons Iotazoon

Mix the passion fruit purée with the Iotazoon in a Thermomix, then heat to 90 °C. Reduce the temperature and with the machine running, add the olive oil in a thin stream as if making mayonnaise.

Coral grouper

1 coral grouper | 30ml lime oil | A little Tempura flour

Fillet the grouper, dust the skin side with Tempura flour and fry quickly in lime oil. Put into the oven and bake for a further 3 minutes at 150 °C, turning only once. Season lightly with salt.

Mangetout

80g mangetout | 30g butter

Cut the mangetout into thin slices and cook in a little water. Glaze with butter and season with a little salt.

To serve

Brioche | Passion fruit seeds | Candied olives | Pimentón

Spoon the sabayon and the mangetout onto a plate. Top with the coral grouper and little bits of brioche. Garnish with passion fruit seeds and candied olives, and sprinkle with Pimentón.

Potato froth with roasted flavour

Potato froth 50g Celluzoon solution | 300g boiled potatoes | 500ml potato water | 10 flattened spoons Algizoon | 30ml olive oil

Celluzoon bath (40 flattened spoons Calazoon and 1 litre water)

To make the Celluzoon solution, whisk 8 flattened spoons Celluzoon into 100ml warm water and store in a fridge over night. Whisk the remaining ingredients together, add the Celluzoon solution and fill into an espuma bottle. Screw on two chargers and spray long lines into the Celluzoon bath. Cut these into pieces and rinse in water. The quantity of Algizoon used in the potato mass has to be adapted to the season.

Roasted flavour 300ml chicken stock | 150g oven-baked potato skins | 2 bay leaves | 1 sprig marjoram

Heat the chicken stock, add the remaining ingredients and poach for 30 minutes. Strain through a sieve and season well.

To serve Marjoram leaves | Toasted croutons

Heat the potato froth in the stock, so that it puffs up. Pour into deep plates. Garnish with bread and marjoram.

Beetroot caviar with blini layer cake

Beetroot caviar with blini layer cake

Beetroot caviar

100ml beetroot juice | 15g Algizoon solution | Pinch of wasabi paste | Pinch of salt | Calazoon bath

Reduce the beetroot juice a little. Whisk in the Algizoon, Wasabi and salt and allow to rest. Draw the mixture up into a syringe and dribble little spheres into the Calazoon bath. Remove after 1 minute. Rinse in a mixture of beetroot juice and water. Hold for no longer than 10 minutes.

Blini layer cake

25g fresh yeast | 500ml milk | 450 wheat flour | 200g buckwheat flour | 25g butter | 100ml cream | 2 eggs | 2tsp sugar | 1tsp salt

200g marinated salmon | 200g sour cream | 1 flattened spoon Locuzoon | A few drops white vinegar

Separate the eggs, whisk the egg whites until stiff. Dissolve the yeast in the milk, then mix with the egg yolks and remaining ingredients. Lastly, fold in the egg whites. Fry small, thin blinis in a frying pan and allow to cool on a rack. This quantity is for more than 4 portions.

Slice the salmon into very thin slices. Bind the sour cream with the Locuzoon and season with the vinegar. Keep a small portion aside for serving, and use the remainder to layer blinis and salmon together. Store in the fridge.

To serve

Borage flowers

Spoon the left-over sour cream decoratively on a plate. Cut the layer cake into portions and lay on top. Add the beetroot caviar and garnish with borage flowers.

Haddock with mustard topping

Haddock

40ml Noilly Prat | Zest of 2 lemons | 30g salt | 4 portions haddock á 40g

Mix the Noilly Prat with the lemon zest and salt. Rub this mixture into the fish and marinate for 8 hours. Remove, pat dry and store covered in oil.

Mustard topping

200ml fish stock | 8 flattened spoons Iotazoon | Fleur de Sel | 30g Dijon mustard seeds | 10g chopped dill

Whisk the Iotazoon into the fish stock, season with salt. Bring to the boil, add the mustard seeds and dill. Stir once and then pour onto a plastic tray. Allow to cool, then cut into pieces the size of the fish portions.

Leek and mustard sauce

1 shallot, diced | 2 pieces of leek, in thin rings | White wine | 100ml chicken stock | 40ml cream | Pinch chlorophyll

Lightly sauté the shallot and leek, deglaze with white wine, then add the stock and cream. Reduce slightly, then mix in the chlorophyll. Sieve and season well.

To serve

5g Dijon mustard seeds | Tomato slivers | In butter sautéed chicory leaves

Pat the haddock dry and top with the mustard mixture. Spoon the leek and mustard sauce around the fish and sprinkle with mustard seeds. Serve with the sautéed chicory leaves and garnish with tomato leaves.

Truffles with cauliflower

Truffles with cauliflower

Cauliflower

1 cauliflower | 1 shallot, diced | 50ml white wine | 20ml chicken stock | 100ml cream | 30g crème fraîche

Set aside 8 small florets from the cauliflower, and finely dice a further 40g. Blanch both separately and set aside. Cut the rest of the cauliflower into small pieces and sauté lightly with the shallot. Deglaze with the white wine, add the stock and cook until soft. Put half into a blender and purée until smooth, adding a little more stock if necessary. Purée the second half and pass through a sieve until really smooth. Whisk in the crème fraîche and season well. Pour into half-moon shaped Silpat forms and put into the freezer.

Truffle stock 200ml veal stock | 50ml truffle stock | 1/2 flattened spoon Xanthazoon | 6 flattened spoons Gellazoon | 3 flattened spoons Locuzoon

Stir the two kinds of stock together. Whisk the Xanthazoon into 50ml of this stock and season well. Mix the Gellazoon and the Locuzoon and whisk into the remaining liquid. Bring to the boil and keep warm at 70 °C. Dip the frozen cauliflower half-moons into this mixture using a skewer. Place onto a tray and allow to thaw. Dip the cauliflower florets also into the mixture and store in the fridge.

To serve 30g truffle in oil | Rock Chives | Light vinaigrette

Cut the truffle into slices, dice and brunoise. Place the cauliflower crème on a plate, top with a half-moon and place the florets decoratively on the side. Garnish with truffle slices and rock chives. Add the truffle dice and spoon over with warm stock. Marinate the diced cauliflower in the vinaigrette and spoon onto the plate. Garnish with truffle brunoise and drizzle with a little stock.

Cranberry air with orange cocktail

Cranberry air

100ml cranberry juice | 30ml cranberry syrup | 2 flattened spoons Emulzoon

Whisk all the ingredients together and then until light and frothy. Allow to stand a little, then scoop off the froth.

Orange cocktail

150g orange fillets | 2tbsp Celluzoon solution | A little honey | 1 drop Rosaria lavender oil

Lay the orange fillets into circles of different dimensions. Season the Celluzoon solution with the honey and lavender oil. Spray this mixture over the orange fillets and heat to 60 °C.

To serve

30ml cranberry purée | Grated rind of 1 lime | Orange zest | Mint brittle | Lavender flowers | Dried cranberries

Place the cranberry purée on a plate and top with a scoop of cranberry air. Arrange the orange cocktail on a plate and top with the grated rind of the lime and the orange zest. Garnish with the mint brittle, lavender flower and dried cranberries.

Physalis with green tea

Green tee 20ml sugar syrup 1:1 | 6 flattened spoons Gellazoon | 3 flattened spoons Locuzoon | 4g Matcha tea

Mix everything together and boil up once. Skim and keep warm.

Physalis 12 physalis

Peel the leaves off the physalis, cut slivers out of the flesh from top to bottom, but not through. Cut a thin slice off the bottom so that the fruit can stand. Put into the freezer until really cold, then dip into the green tea to glaze the fruit. Stand the physalis on a rack to drain.

To serve 12 physalis | 40g mango purée | Chopped pistachios

Cut each physalis into eight pieces and marinate in the mango purée. Serve on a plate topped with the chopped pistachios. Garnish with the physalis.

Soft mango jelly with mango salad

Soft mango jelly

100ml mango juice | 20ml mango purée | 5ml white vinegar | 6 flattened spoons Iotazoon | 20g sugar | Zest of 1 lime

Mix the mango purée, juice and vinegar, then add the Iotazoon. Bring to the boil. Pour onto Silpat sheets and put in the fridge to get cold. Dust with sugar and lime zest before serving.

Mango salad

60g mango | 20g barberry berries | 10g pistachios | 20g mango purée

Cut the mango into squares, the barberry berries and pistachios into slices. Mix with the mango purée and season to taste.

To serve

Mango slices | Mango sauce | Vanilla air | Barberry berry sauce

Place the mango jelly, mango salad and mango slices on a plate. Add the mango sauce and the barberry berry sauce. Serve with a portion of vanilla air (Prepare as the coffee froth on page 51, but without the coffee beans, anise and cardamom).

Running out of texturizers?

No more droppers or pipettes?

They can all be ordered

from the following addresses:

biozoon food innovations gmbh
Fischkai 1
27572 Bremerhaven (Germany)

Phone	00 49 (0) 4 71 - 48 32 404
Fax	00 49 (0) 4 71 - 48 32 419
Mail	info@biozoon.de
Internet	www.biozoon.de/shop

In Austria:
RAPS GmbH, Gewürzwerk

Phone	00 43 (0) 62 19 - 75 57 - 0
Fax	00 43 (0) 62 19 - 75 57 - 85
Mail	bestellservice@raps.at
Internet	www.raps.at

In Switzerland:
freestylecooking GmbH

Phone	00 41 (0) 32 - 652 16 01
Mobile	00 41 (0) 78 - 682 00 87
Mail	info@freestylecooking.ch
Internet	www.freestylecooking.ch

To find out more about the wide variety of applications of molecular cuisine beyond "Molecular Basics", we recommend the following books:

Heiko Antoniewicz / Klaus Dahlbeck

Verwegen kochen

Molecular techniques and texturizers

ISBN 978-3-87515-024-7

Heiko Antoniewicz

Fingerfood

Culinary art at its very best

ISBN 978-3-87515-015-5

Awarded the Gourmand World Cookbook Award as "Best Innovative Cookbook in the World"

Awarded a Gold Medal by the Gastronomischen Akademie Deutschlands e.V.

More information: www.matthaes-shop.de

Alphabetical Recipe Index

Savoury

Sweet

Recipe index according to groups

Spherification

Foams

Gelling

Thickeners

Combined agents

Heiko Antoniewicz

Born 1965 in Dortmund, Heiko Antoniewicz has consolidated his first-rate status as chef in the course of the last 20 years in various positions.
Today he is CEO of Antoniewicz GmbH. He is advisor to many companies in both the gastronomy sector and food industries regarding product development and quality management. He is internationally renowned for his seminars and cooking courses where he passes his extensive knowledge on to professional chefs and hobby cooks alike.
His passion for innovative themes and extraordinary, surprisingly uncomplicated recipes is visible in all his books. They have all become bestsellers, have received awards, some of them even the coveted "Best in the World" award.

www.verwegen-kochen.de,
www.antoniewicz.org, ha@antoniewicz.org

Ralf Müller

Born 1960 in Binzen, Ralf Müller studied photo design at Dortmund University. During his studies he set up the company "CENTRUM – Sudio für Fotografie" with some of his colleagues. The broad spectrum of the work of his studio includes the creation of visual designs and photographic assignments focussing on advertising, stills, people, industry and food.

Ralf Müller, Fotographie, Overhoffstraße 2,
44379 Dortmund, www.rmfd.de, info@rmfd.de

René Bastian Stein

Born 1981 in Hagen, he trained to become a chef from 1998 to 2001 in the Landhaus Syburg restaurant in Dortmund. After a first posting in Freiburg, he worked with Heiko Antoniewicz from 2002 to 2004 as Art Manager in Dortmund before joining Martin Göschel at the Tiger Palast in Frankfurt where he stayed for two years. He worked as Chef de Partie for Juan Amador in Langen from 2006 to May 2008.

Thorsten kleine Holthaus

Born 1982 in Braunschweig, he worked as assistant to the photographer Marc Stantien in Braunschweig before studying Photo Design at Dortmund University in 2004, where he focused on advertising photography. He has been working for Karin Hessmann and Ralf Müller at "CENTRUM – Studio für Fotografie" alongside his studies since 2006.

Frieder Krohmer

Born 1969 in Reutlingen, he studied graphic design at the "Akademie-Fellbach für Grafik-Design" and then went on to gain experience with various advertising agencies. In 1993 he set up his own graphic design studio with his wife. At the beginning he concentrated on classical advertising, but today he deals more with the design of books and book covers, including typesetting.

Atelier Krohmer, Kommunikations-Design,
www.atelierkrohmer.de

Imprint

ISBN 978-3-87515-034-6

Recipes and foodstyling: Heiko Antoniewicz, Bergkamen
Photography: Ralf Müller Fotografie, CENTRUM, Dortmund
Translation: Beatrix Davies-Labeck, www.labeck.eu
Editor: Martina Kunrath, Stuttgart
Graphic design and production: Atelier Krohmer, Dettingen/Erms

Printed in Germany

Note This contents of this book have been carefully researched and tested, however no guarantee is given for the contents thereof. Neither the author, the publisher nor any persons or institutions instructed by them assume any responsibility for personal, material or pecuniary damage resulting from it use.